Growing Down

Growing Down

J. Pittman McGehee

INK
BRUSH
PRESS

ISBN: 978-0-9883839-8-2
Library of Congress Control Number: 2012956493

Front Cover Art: Merrilee McCommas McGehee
Back Cover Photograph: Deborah Hardee
Manufactured in the United States

Ink Brush Press
Temple and Dallas

For

My wife, Bobby

Sons,
Pittman and Jarrett

Daughters-in-law
Merrilee and Leigh Ann

Grandchildren
Finnegan, Baxter, Clementine, Quinton

(Poetry in Motion)

Acknowledgments

I am grateful to Merrilee McCommas McGehee, my very creative artist daughter-in-law, for her outstanding cover design.

This book would not have been published without the insightful help and expertise of my gifted administrative assistant, Cathy Trull Jenkins.

Thanks to Jerry Craven, press director of Ink Brush Press for his finding me and my poetry and for his pleasant, efficient, and professional manner.

I appreciate the editors of these journals and anthologies for publishing some of the poems in this collection: *The Saint Luke's Journal of Theology, Cite Magazine, Paraclete Press, i.e. Magazine, Anglican Theological Review, Cimarron Review, Houston Poetry Fest Anthology, Windhover,* and *New Texas.*

CONTENTS

Shofar

"Get thee out of thy country, and from thy
birthplace and from thy father's house, unto a
land that I show thee." —Genesis 12:1

O sad call for joy, awaiting sacred
sounds through desert waste, mud-oven
and scaffold sea. No different, we
who listen still, heeding the glass
breaking voice, pitched too high to
hear, and yet distinct. Discernment
comes in small morsels, just enough
for a tender moment, a tentative step.

Call me. To be. Out. From. Unto,
to be shown only when lost and insecure.
Thirst, I know, even though I drink,
hunger cuts my belly full and I want
more than my country or father can now
loan. Alone, to be shown, by silence.

Point, beyond itself—symbol sound,
life flight, wild goose, thunder roll,
whirlwind, water spout, "Get thee out!"

Where are you?
Have you seen the shoram or heard the
horn? I am told we must move on and

lean against the know falling up
ward toward the not known, holding
in our hands the severed string,

1

translucent and cut in curls. How
long can we wait before we are told
we stayed too long and never broke
the now, or wet our feet, or pierced
the sacred soil with our heel?

How I dread the bite of sand and
honey and fear not to have known
its taste against my tongue and teeth.

Obey

The song is in the egg before
the bird is born. All creation
waits with one collective
vow of obedience to listen
for the time when the creature
will sing the singular sound
for which he was created.

Paz Says

"Love is a victory over time..."

Sometimes I can't quite
quiet the primitive, the
part not so free, beneath
radiant rays, where dusk
holds musk. Shadows
mesh like mist and
cover any hope that this
love will win.

The body thickens slack
changing shape like a
fluid in a sack: Mercury
sad. The only word is
temporal, sight without sound,
no finger tips or nostrils.
Tasteless. So now, my pal
Paz, where is the irrational
power audacious enough
to save my abandonment?

4

Omena Bay

has roadside stands.
Berries, blue and rasp,
in small wooden baskets
are beside the cherries,

sweet and sour. Just
like an August years
ago, a satin cardinal
flew after his mate

creating a duet, flush
and full. Somewhere
near, there must be a deer
leaping. I pay a

cigar box in honor of
the system and turn
toward the light
breaking through the birch.

Conifer

In the piney woods
cones grow lips and
spin like tops. Organisms
enact sacrifice. Needles
make beds for fawns. Seeds
seed. Bears scratch backs
on rough bark. Trees
house. Leaves are flying
carpets for ants. And

even now there are
two who interplay,
merge, circle, break
down walls. There in
the pine is the good
pain, natural, symmetrical
ensouled in feathers,
formerly wings.

Ash Wednesday

On Huron, down Bad River we
fished for walleye with worm
harnesses and bass on artificial
lures, tent living, rock life, moss
mortar anchored pegs in pores.
Lake water and blended whiskey
swirling in a tin cup smells
like the sound of six Brandenburgs
by Bach. Swimming buck naked in
the cold, crystal rock-bottom hole
behind the blueberry bushes where
bears come when the inland crops are
bad and laughing at egrets with legs
long like orange straws, we savored
the fish fried in peeled onions
with skinned potatoes. Heaven.
Except for the mosquitoes who
come in their little brown fogs,
waiting for the sky to pink up and
the clouds to blue, then leave
with the first cool breeze.

Last Game At The Park

Do the birds sing this morning, or is it a memory?
Some say the sky is gray, but it's white.
The geese have flown into the moon and
There is a lovely sound of their discontent.
The rains will soon be snow and
As the trees turn black, the
Flowers go back down.
Now, the truth becomes visible:
Beauty is camouflaged in death.

The architect of the soul shows through.
God removes a coat of colors and
Is at home with us.
We return to what lies beneath the
Beauty, and remember our lives.
We will not hurry.
We will make love in time.
For now, time puts down roots
And comes back year after year.

Montrose Moon

God must love the Montrose:
the mountain and the flower.

In Advent the moon and
earth moved into their closest embrace.

When the lunar hug held
the world, shadows stilled.

God was present, barely visible,
silver. She moved there.

No, Known

And so I've been curious,
about the sounds of no and known.

So much of life has been centered around the no,
Setting the boundary and barrier,
Living the ethic. Making the decide:
You know, suicide, homicide.

But, now to be known.
The conditions are different.

To be known with the leaves
blowing their own way.
To be known like the shine of dew
on a new day's lawn.
To be known in the fullest, the deepest
and the longing.

This is where things are in soft focus.
Where nothing is eroded.
The more it is seen the more it grows.

I would be happy at this time to be known
Where the bones are,
Where the meaning is,
Where the deepest curves of the body's map
lead to a new geography.

To be known.
To never say no again.

A Slice of Life

It was just a slice of life
when the silver wings cut
through the blue tower and
tore our soul in two.

I was struck by the birds
who flew from the smoke
and dust. In the crash of
glass, wings fluttered up.

Context

Corrugated tin forms,
like cardboard turned in-
side out hiding light in
gray waves, were the
ubiquitous buildings of my youth,
leaving no more impression
than bald mesquite or
barbed wire.

In 1969, I saw this
Walker Evans image. Like a
Masai warrior seeing a
Serengeti lion on
Broadway, I saw my life on the
MOMA wall.

Something rose, while the
tin lion yawned, and I
fell prey.

Ring the Broken Pail

Retell the story once again
  not for those who did not hear,
  but for those who never knew.
How the silent hand grasped the nail
  and fell across the tree.
How the Eden vine was cut
  and tore the tattered veil.
How upon the Holy Grail
  the wine was shed by drops.
Pause beneath the wounded wing
  and ring the broken pail.

Who will thorn the bird
  and scream the song as sung?
Where's the warming fire this night
  to burn denial's tongue?
Grow the rose once more
  and pull its petals bare.
Climb up on the singletree
  and tell of truth's despair.

Drumright, OK 1952

Crouched on porch steps counting cars.
Waiting. Mother smokes on the
crushed velvet sofa rubbing her
legs. Cellophane, clear and stretched
tight on the empty package: Camels.
Brother builds a model plane. Match
sticks, toothpicks, balsa. Tedious,
tentative. Focused, furrowed brow
step by step. Patience. Unaware
of time. Tissue paper taut.
The dust feels moist on the cracked
concrete. Sheba rolls in the mud by
the sunflowers: dog days. Cat-eyed car
lights come on slowly then fade fast.
Sidewalk stone tossing, pacing up and
down. Fireflies fight for dark in the
street light and time is a night train.

Higher Than Time

Have you not dreamed of what wheels
freely as laughter winged and flung
higher than time? The faultless
halls of air dare not pause for
we will tumble past: upward.

The Years Are Many Any Now

This is the timorous season.
Irreversible continuum of time
star crossed thoughts of Christ-
mas eve driving home alone.

The incense of sky is stippled
silent lights. The streets
are wet ash. Now shadows
dream misty joy and lonely

grief. A crocus to be delivered
as a midnight sachet sits
beside me now lush
and come of age. Eyes

are apertures, every sight
a memory and a dream. The
silhouettes intersect to-
circulate the intervals and

oscillate the time as birth
and when alone to know
that every year and there are
many now, moves us closer

to the shameless sunrise coming
from a sleeping source resting
still in a rough hewn bed waiting
for the sacred fire to light.

Traveling Man

When Euchee Creek flooded it
kept Daddy home. Cut off from
Cushing he couldn't work
the territory so he took
my brother and me in the "any
color you want as long as it's

black" Ford. Past the drive-in
theater, the tourist court
was vacant at the top of the hill.
Down below, the creek had
swallowed the bridge and

gone to sleep over the corn
field. A cow floated slowly
by, bloated and blown up
like a boxing glove. A gasoline
truck was stuck just where

the highway died. Water underlined
"flammable" on the round
tank side. My brother
wondered how and I asked why?
Dad wore a thin white shirt,

gabardine pants and a pair of
spectator shoes, brown and
white. His glasses were rimmed
in wire and his face was frozen
in a sun grin as he watched
the water and held my hand till it hurt.

Incarnation

Snow fell on the hill all
night long before I rolled
out of bed, wrapped in my
outing flannel, figured with
Roy Roger's face and Trigger.

Open faced gas stove honored the
Oklahoma winter, and icicles hung
from the roof lines scarring the snow
blanket below. I screamed. Brother
bundled me in a blanket, saved my

life, at eight. Flesh burned and
blistered three degrees deep hung
round my legs like sagging, silk
stockings. No ambulance could come
in spite of a mother's shriek so shrill

as to break the glass hill holding
us hostage. A limp body laid
upon a bed by a frightened
father, paternal pieta faltered
in shock as tremors shook a

boy struggling to become seven.
Semi-conscious. Conversation
covered me like the white cotton
sheet she smoothed for my berth.
"Call the doctor!" Orange Star,

who had gone away to study healing.
Creek County's only medicine man and
snow bound too. My daddy's black
Ford skated on the hill and it would
have been a game except for the pain.

They leaned against the wind, brisk
steps breaking the brittle icing.
The physician, tall with a plow
horse's girth and hair, a shock of
white wheat. Black bag with O. Star

M.D. carried morphine, salvation in
a syringe. And she, Mary the nurse,
burst blisters, water balloons,
scalpelled with silver scissors, sliced
the membranes, trimmed the proud flesh.

For Father Louis

We are already one. Now is
our journey toward that unity
which we have known, yet
never held close. Like
short lived lovers.

Here we are discovering the
recovery of our original
union. Becoming who we are
now born to be. Come with
me on the plane beyond words

where speech is smoke, breath
is fire, and water falls on
time. Sacred space: an
infinite point holding all the
poets' verses in a universe that

is speechless, wordless and one.

Domine, Deus

Squirrels on strong hind legs pause
nervously and grasp for one more
morsel. Staring an eye-corner
stare at winter's approach through
the fall, and piles leave wind-
blown crackling under soles walking
across the gray grass toward the
time of raw-boned bitterness where,
only months before leaves flourished
green with chlorophyll.

Winter's raw edge cuts close in a
contemplative walk. Squirrels watch
from hidden holes, natural gift of knowing—
the tree is safe for animals.
The change of season calls out the
colors: burnt orange and red, yellow
in brilliance before death, now brown
by frost's first silver blade. No
photosynthesis, no, not any is seen
by squirrels and shattered

remnants are left to be ground down
by souls journeying across the year
to court a warm spot safe from winter's
chill. Death through the fall leaves
leaves like ashes scattered. Where are
the birds? Flown like smoke and cries
of absence. Some sing psalms by day and
night, awaiting the snow cover over the
grave and the sun to give light

to those who sit in darkness, in
the shadow of death.

Credo

"And for all this, nature is never spent;
    There lives the dearest freshness deep down things;

And though the last lights off the black West went
    Oh, morning, at the brown brink eastward, springs—

Because the Holy Ghost over the bent
    World broods with warm breast and with ah! bright
        wings."
                    —Gerard Manley Hopkins

I believe in the resurrection because
when I hear the story in sacred language
and divine liturgy I feel it to be
making known what is true, felt down deep
where things begin. Something
wells up to awareness, a spirit,
a primordial spirit, like a brown brink
emerging out of darkness until
something signals a Holy Spirit that existed
before me and dwells within.
These deep down things emerge
above horizon and remain fixed,
seared and sealed in consciousness, and
no darkness can hide these
things that arise again. And again.

Where the Watercress Grows

The click too sharp. The
clack too flat. Each an abrupt
dry sound. Scornful
clucking slack tongues of
pseudo-sagacity. The
children are called by some
inarticulate, ancient sound
to play in the mud.

Dirt? Yes. More so earth.
Mud? And water from a
font spring found as
a land loch where
naked trifles gambol
curious and innocent.
Moist, earthen laughter, somer-
saults and slides: fluid motion.

Gargoyles sit at gutters and
carry rain water clear
of the wall. Dust
dancing with drops from
Cathedral roofs. Flumes leading
streams down to pools where
watercress grows wild and sumptuous.

A Run Away

I remember Mavis Melcher on smokey
mornings.
She lived across from Dexter Estes on Elm,
which ran the ridge above the hollow where
Dr. Ard's stud pranced nervously when Mavis
passed by. Her pink sweater was a cotton
bathed valley with maiden form peaks bouncing
as she and Shirley Kyle walked on ahead of
us. They were fourteen and we ten when honey
suckle blankets hung on barbed wire like
wreaths around a thoroughbred's neck in the
winner's circle.

Dexter Estes let the stud loose one noon
day, and he broke for the wild side, flanks
flexed as he followed the tracks under the
willows toward Tulsa. The vision of sun
flowers and the smell of freshly mown alfalfa
was muddled by dust rings and flared nostrils.
His mane stood the wind and his tail sailed
behind. Several stories circulated about
his capture and Mavis Melcher told the girls,
"You can't trust the boys."

My brother threw a rock into the horse
barn and it echoed against the corrugated
tin: a sharp sound and then silence.

Blues

[If] "Words Were Invented to Hide Feelings,"

Then why do the
poets use
blues to paint
bright skies and
dark moods?

Waist deep in the
surf my son and
I baited hooks
with shrimp and
landed brown
speckled trout.
A blue heron
flew unattested
crosscutting the
intracoastal water
way. The boy's
tanned skin was
stretched tight by
his bent arm,
holding the flue
high and full
of the dapple,
thrashing
strength for strength
bent against his
biceps, flexed
full to the elbow.
Beer and bice

crabs sat well against
a long day's tide.
From the South the
wind blew, a rhapsody
of dreams in rhythm
with the young
man's breath and
I lay on the twin
adrift in the
beryl night.

A Vision of Angels

The fire, horror hidden, transpired
through the years. Like a child
creating a cradle from a broken
box, I have played upon the scars
like a black butterfly lost in night's
slackness, the flame unaware but there
flickering in the captured laughter
of a missed youth born out of season.
The smoldering heat appeared in beach
sand as smokeless powder.

In a summer chill, I grasped a blanket,
shelter from the shadowed cold. Seeing
the water, I longed for sea circles,
quiescent until now. And dreamed
death's dream of burnt lips, salivating
thirst, tasting the cotton which grew
like cedars bearing fruit out of season
and withering in the evergreen. Like
Jacob I knew nothing then and knew it
all too soon:

a desert cactus bloom, alone, no one
to see how I imagined even then the
end from when it all began. The vesper
tears, seawalls broken like salt stained
cracked cheeks when lanquid tongues whisper
passion's dry chant. I will not know the
pain again, never again to hurt as when
the hot coral kissed my naked leg and

my soul screamed bare forsaken ecstasy
on the brink of life's first inspiration.

Living for a while on bread and a little wine
I read and gave myself away in the aura
of candles and torch lit processions. But
the sullen dark held the terror of the tidal
roar. Sea circles curled up out of a votive
light in a covenant without time, promising a
new taper, tender, trustful, wedding the
world, shouting for the season yet to come.
Coming and still to be, the wild strawberry
the aria of the lily two trumpets to a stem.

Day Trip

The old yellow wagon, rusted at the running
boards, smelled of mold and mildew, growth and
decay. Green powder dusted the paint, paper,
plastic cloth, leather and the like. Asexual
spores, microorganisms growing unnoticed
seducing all matter in a sporadic, verdant
mist. She talked of needlepoint and
cottage curtains. The air was cordial, but
brittle, boding of sweaters and fires at
dark. The broken barn served as a silent
haymow. Auburn grass cut and dried,
bound, hollow stems, rolled, set aside for
fodder when the graze had drifted white.
The meadow below was two levels of lavender,
thistle and clover. A cherry orchard made
round shadows that fashioned a dark, sacred
grove. The fruit of the bitter sweet
sanctuary was heart shaped with a stone
center.

The moment passed like all the mail boxes,
tattooed with letters and red cedars cast
long fingers across the glass. Our vision
fluttered in the distance as we drove on
toward the shore.

Pegasus

Autry had no access to justice. His
life fell before him like lumber
cut at random and stacked pell-
mell in his path. His jacket

had genuine leather sleeves, black with
red wool panels. A "W" stitched over
his heart was grease-stained. I
used to fill my tire with air and

watch him flirt with Shirley Kyle. Her
jeans were rolled up, her socks down
and she wore her daddy's shirt-tail
out. Against the pump her breasts

were silhouetted like turnips
through the white cotton. Gas
stations were educations. Mr.
Nester told me, "not to hang around

them older boys," but he also told
me dirty jokes and didn't seem to mind
my curiosity about his pin-up calendar.
Learned a lot that summer, more than

I knew. When school started Autry
grew a mustache and joined the Navy.
Told me he "couldn't play ball any
more so he was off to see the world."

My big brother saw him hitch
hiking out toward the Fond

du Lac. Korea. First time I heard
the word. Peninsula. Inchon.

Mother peeled potatoes over a news
paper, drainboard spread. "Autry T.
Mann killed in action." Backpage
picture in uniform. I rode my

bike by the Mobil and saw
the flying red horse. It was
dusk and the wind blew the bone
gray vines on Dr. Neil's board fence.

I circled by Washington School,
navigating the cracked walk, down past
the police station and peddled
up Tiger Hill as fast as I could

to slide under Mother's clothes-
line before dark and bury myself
under the quilts left to flap
clean in the crisp fall breeze.

Waiting in an Airport Lounge

Of all places the clock on the
wall was stopped. I mused,
at least twice a day it was
exactly right.

I looked to my wrist. As
far as I know my watch
has never been correct.

I will choose the living
reality over the dead certainty.

August Fire

Like natives we called it "The Point."
I can still see her eyes when she
saw the shingled cottage through the split-
railed fence.

She knew that I knew we had been there before—
in stories written about the rich and famous.
Fitzgerald and Cheever taught us of sailboats
and summer sand.

That year I built my first August fire and
ate a breakfast of fresh raspberries and cream.
A Quaternity of boys sailed sunfishes and drove
little boats.

We sat together against the chill and saw the moonrise.
It was orange and black and walked across the water
on a copper path. The midnight moon played a
lover's tune on its bays of floating clouds.

Our minds ran with our feet and I
looked for a face in the asphalt.
Once again, I looked in the wrong place.
We ran a corridor of pine trees with a blue
ribbon above. I didn't see God, but
I think He saw me. She wore purple.

That night I slept with my lover of years.
This year we heard water sounds and
a bell buoy ringing the limit of time.

Movement

Windows wet with rain frame a
misty image of a lone magnolia
blossom, pure white, waved
back and forth by a
black wand,

free from any responsibility to the
green grass or mossy brick below.

Light reflected, deflected down toward
all that was born to set a stage
for this opalescent moment in time

when I would see through a rain-wet
window the bloom, white pure
presented this day for me.
Magnificent magnolia.

Blanche Fleur

Hard-boned, flesh fingers, hand-
planted bulbs. Knee knelt before
the bed, watered now in

irony. Blanche Fleur, rising
truth in the fall seeking
words, written on paper white.

God writes messages in stories
lived and told in quiet talks,
matter of fact miracle. Simple

time when things come circle
connected like holding held
for another time. Just. Now,

this single truth: these
blossoms grieve, for this time
is not full grown.

Vietnam Memorial

It seemed to be a "V" for a black victory near
the White House where

Lincoln sat and watched as I looked
for my friend's name.

Washington stood erect as a monumental
witness to the impotence of

the Vietnam war. Black rock spreads
itself out to the voyeurs searching

for a victory by finding a friend's name
who died once again

in vain.

Baptism

The northern lights reflected on
the waters making known what
was already true.

And the father guarded the water that first
night. We knew his spirit would move us
as the wind and make the family one.

Meaning, purpose and belonging came
together in a synchronous touch.
Drops of lake water fell from young
heads and tears from older eyes.

The world was still real, differences were
not reconciled. Peace passed understanding.

It would always be a drop
of truth reflecting the
unknown.

Hope

The harpsichord. Designed to play
with strawberries and champagne.
Unless a gift comes like a gracious
seed in the wind the wood remains
untouched by the craftsman's hands.

The grapes have yet to appear on
the vine and the berry blossoms
are felt only by hidden stems,
not yet healthy enough to appear
above ground.

The words are written to be read
to harpsichord tunes. Eating
strawberries and drinking champagne
will come in the fullness of time.
The seeds are in the wind.

Cocktails

I entertained the circle with clever lines of tree crows
cawing and seagulls clanging like bell buoys.

Bill Romey whispered that they were ravens. "Ravens eat
fish," he said. "More poetic." I smiled.

Dody Romey had a stroke last summer. Her face
is like an apple cut in half and put back
uneven. "She looked it up in a bird book," said Bill.
She smiled. "Ravens. They are ravens," he repeated
and patted his wife's crossed hands.

It was a moment. Only an instant. A fleeting
small thread of a moment. "Ravens." She
must have pointed to the page supporting her
limp left hand with her right. "Ravens,"
he said. She smiled. I smiled back.

Dody Romey knew. Bill said, "They eat fish."
They were not crows. They were ravens.

Susan's Wall

Brown and darker brown, rust, rose, and
red squares, light and gray mortar
draw long lines and short ones down.
A cross. Worn a bit and waved away
from strict, straight rules drawn by
builder and brick mason. Form and
function: no clearer than shadow
lines faint with age.

Walled in and out standing
between here and there. Brick
walls—red and brown barriers
seeking boundaries, limits, definite
definition. Tumbling in
time, leaving us without
space. Boarders without rooms,
room without borders—gray lines.

No Present Like the Time

Truth rests not in the broad upland of,
"We have only to live for today." The
present is the narrow ridge of the
eternal now, the only moment. Memory
and imagination, bookends of time,
moving from then to when. We have
rainbows that promise golden ends grasped
where truth is too deep as to keep the

future completeness forever. Tastes.
Foretastes, tempt us to take control,
and yet we know we are known as a chosen
people. Promised, and unwilling to live
tomorrow when this is but a heartbeat
in the only history we have. Essence in
existence is our ecstasy. Still, we wait
in time having been given everything.

New Harmony, Indiana

Bird breast orange amongst the brown furrows
flies low across the field, fertility groaning
in shoots against the odds. Out of dust
becoming, unconscious and inevitable, sown
in rows of unknown endings not seen but
believed by those who broadcast the seed.

The Blessing of a Dream

The archetypal cock crowed
me into consciousness at the light of day.

My father looked so natural in my mother's kitchen
and the blessed smell of coffee called to me.

His skin was white coveralls with
blue stripped veins. Hair of
thin spider's silk, a graceful walk
disguised within a shuffle,
his face, a piece of driftwood:
weathered wisdom.

"What are you worried about," he said.
My silence suffered.
He shuffled.
"Whatever it is, don't worry. It'll be okay."

And I received his blessing
in a common cup of coffee.

Morning Song

Psalm 42

"As the deer longs for the
waterbrooks, so longs my
soul for you."
So wrote the psalmist re-
ferring to his desire for
God.

As I read that psalm this day
I, of course, thought of us:
you, me, we.

I pulled on my socks and
put on the water. Toasted and
buttered my bread, then
tasted the richness.

I don't know the difference
between longing for God
and longing for you.

Pilates

You gotta love an
exercise where bed of
torture is called a,
reformer.

Straps, pulleys, springs,
hooks, all designed to
inflict pain in a drawn
and quartered kinda way.

It is a stretch, but
my instructor is the
world's smallest sadist.
Of course, you know that

makes me the world's
largest masochist. My
safe word is, "Pomegranate,"
a many-seeded fruit.

So this is a poetic
confession, that I
have been reformed and
transformed.

Standing straighter,
squatting deeper, my
core is confirmed, firmer.
Glutes, quads, abs,
less pliable and

my body/soul more
integrated. It is the
paradox of pain and
pleasure, not totally
in that perverted way.

Pilates, you gotta
love an exercise whose
trapeze of terror
is called a "Cadillac."

He Told Me Not to Cling

He vanished. My soul left empty
like the tomb. "Do not
hold..." the sound of his
words, were powerful like
the sea when her tide
flows away.

He must be found in the
vacant place, not behind the
rock, but within the heart.
He left to now be known in-
side. Edged out of the world
on a tree, like the first
at Eden—now a new
creation—a new way to
be known in the deep.
The man disappears as
the divine reappears in-
side those who have
the eye to see.

Where to go with this
wealth that holds no earthly
value? Can I slide
seamlessly back into my
ordinary life? How to serve
him now? The garden is
green in the morning light.
The angels have departed
and I too must leave like
Eve before me. Innocence

is gone and the world
is full of labor, pain and
death. And yet...

I set my table with a
loaf, and a little wine.
Break open a pomegranate
and taste its red seed. I
contemplate an aura of
candles and wait for the
bridegroom to return
here and to appear...
amidst the aria of
the lily, two trumpets
to a stem.

Indianola, July 4

Leroy and I had chased
fish for twenty years.
Reds and specks eluded

our lures that day, so we took
dark beer in frosty bottles
and guided each other

toward our ancestral
graves at Indianola.

Head stones:

> Young Charles Chadwick
> taken by the yellow fever
> "all flesh is grass."
> 1840 - 1849

his cracked, tan face tilted
toward the sea when I asked,
"Have we honored these folks?"

We drove by rusted Air-
streams and cinder block
houses. Old dogs, rib-

lined, scratched by the
scruffy mesquite. "I dunno,"
he said, "I dunno."

Vox Deo

Some say they have never
had a religious experience.
I ask, "Have you never seen
a baby born, or had a dream?"

The ordinary becomes the extra-
ordinary. Dreams. Who knows?
They compensate, inspire,
threaten, entertain, reveal.

Where do they come from?
Mystery. Could it be from
the unconscious? From
God? What is the

difference? *Vox Deo.*
We hear the voice of
God in the ordinary
laughter of grandchildren,

in the sun lit yellow
rose in an ordinary office.

I was at the birth of my
second son. Dream, mystery
where did he really come from?
I called my five year old
first born and told
him I had a second son.
He cried out, "I was
praying for a brother."

Could that be the voice
of God? Birth, prayer,
dream, mystery. Some
say they have never had

a religious experience.

The Origin and Nature of Egocentricity

Pick and roll, double post, weave, baseline,
backboard, jump shot, free throw. No less
sinewy than the pallid, drawn Bolshoi
androgynes, whose choreography is practiced
and precise, except here with spontaneity in

tights, squared and sleeveless, a boy, a
star, inflated for coordination, ordained to
entertain plays to win.

Jump, run, handle the ball, shoot your eyes
out. Rules, discipline, one hundred percent.
Metaphor: the game of life.

The aging, colossus finds his stunted growth
in the vicious cycle of the victor's circle:
avoid defeat, no other goals.

The more he strives, the fear increases, the
exertion grows, the limbs tremble, the heart
quickens, and breaking faster: defeat.

All sovereignty, all superiority, all security,
and high hopes fall down for what remains is the
pampered, the cherished hero, miserable,
expendable, whose lead legs and flaccid arms,
beg for mercy like a clinging vine.

11-04-08

Dr. King's dream found
flesh in Grant Park.
Oprah cried ancestral
tears. Our shame turned
to joy. Heads were not
bowed in prayer, but
held high in order to
smell the redolent in-
cense of sacrifice and
to see the unfettered
smile of freedom.

Deaths

The first time I saw my father cry,
we'd buried my infant sister. Red
clay pretended to be dirt at his
feet. Grass was brown. Green was
dead: an overdose of
Oklahoma sun.

From the back his shoulders shook, no
different than the windblown prairie brush.
His head moved from side to side. I
never saw the tears. He wiped them
away, perhaps from shame, but the grass
needed all the help it could get.

Denying the mid-morning summer sun, my
brother stood at attention. Male
model. Military. Mother cried
alone and men buried her only
girl. From the empty room she stared
out through a broken pane and one son sees

still. The last time I saw my father cry
we were sweating and grass was brown.

Why We Have Bodies

My son, when four, once asked:
"Why do we have bodies?"

I said, "to locate our souls,
to identify that of another, to
experience our soul's located
in time and space.

After all,
it is so we can know the subtle
and sublime, the pore, the soft
coarseness of hair, the hard nail,
the soft flesh, the color pink
and brown, that which merges
to purple when the blue vein
and the pink skin meet.

It is to know God after all
how else will we experience
grace, except in the law of the
body? The body's law is ecstasy."

Jarrett's Poem

My last son's hair shines in the light,
the color of distant wheat.

His body is little-boy boney and brown.
When he walks the grass prays for grace.

His eyes reveal truth in advent blue.
He blinks and the world turns a turn.

Gold, brown, blue. I hear those
colors in bursts of laughter.

Son bursts.

Fifth Birthday

Give me your rough edges or I will
take them.

Your personality dances behind brown
eyes and a straight-toothed smile,
an electric hobby horse
turning and burning.

The temptation is twofold:
Fear the fire and mold the mystery
as you burn in some easy peace.

Turn and burn blonde beautiful one.
Your flame cannot be extinguished
either by you or me.
Manhood awaits you only if
you don't grow up.

Summer '78

The baby danced with his shadow on the
wall. He and I saw it and knew it was
important. We've been constant companions
dancing with shadows from shared minds
refusing to be embarrassed by expressed love.

We ran to eat long sandwiches and long
neck bottles poured out laughter at
sacramental meals.

We dressed up like old men and went to
lunch like pretty women and talked grown-up
talk and giggled at our shadows on the wall.

Summer shadows grow short in long winter's
nights, but written memories warm.

Limited Updike

A summer garden party complete with
fireflies and pink crepe myrtle I talked
of literature, wore white linen and
tried to be a Southern writer, smelled of
whiskey and wrote of incest

and insanity. The tall woman with chiseled
cheeks wasn't impressed with my limited
Updike. It came to me like a night-light
on a white blossom and lasted as long as
the ice in my julep:

Cynicism is the other side of idealism—
two headed coin with no common metal.
I couldn't even write home for a while.
So I taught my children vowel sounds and
kissed their pursed lips.

Insight

The bay, gray with early fog offers only
sounds. A boat circles slowly searching for
its dock, shaving a bow-wake heard on the
shore, unseen.

A bell buoy echoes a cadence uneven
against the gull's grand laughter and
taunts the crow's call against
the mist.

Crickets, confused by obscurity, make
night sounds early. Frog throats signal
lake life and fish seeking insects splash
water rings.

When the opaque blanket hides the bay, a
stoney point sits in silence and awaits
the appearance of the
summer sun.

To William Carlos Williams

Write with abandon and
abandon the word for another
is called to complete the
work. It is a machine

of perpetual motion. Every
word plays its part and
no redundant thought rolls
over again apart from the

whole. Well-oiled movement,
evolving eternally, gaining
momentum into a final line
left alone for now.

Five and Dime

At the dime store watches stopped
dead until the clerk would revive
them with a shake. Where are the
windup watches? No more rituals
of winding and settling, or
listening for life in a heart beat
or a bent wrist.

And where was she? I lost my mama
searching for time, looked up and
she was gone and I pretended
I wasn't crying walking across
the hardwood floors, warped
with wear to the hot sidewalk
that burned my bare feet.

They've put batteries inside men. So
where will the poets be now that
the moon has been walked on and the
heart beats artificially? Metaphors
of my childhood are machines, but
life continues, motion in poetry and
feet cooled in the mud.

Mentor

Odysseus' trusted guide was
named Mentor. In the Greek
menos means passion or purpose.
Mentors help mentees find
their path.

I have had many mentors.
Passion, purpose, path
with generous guides showing
the way. I now mentor and
suffered the illusion that
at my age I could not
have another guide.

Then my first grandson was
born. He is my mentor,
teaching me to live more fully.
He thinks not of the past or future,
but travels fully in the present.

He feels his feelings and
speaks the truth. He needs not
impress, nor seduce.
He is curious, spontaneous
and innocent.

I have grown up,
I am now growing down.
Unless I become like
this child, I cannot enter
the kingdom.

The Weaver and the Woven

She spins a mandala.
Simultaneously, I listen to
stories. Out the window
behind their minds, as a
spider weaves a web.

July's amber turns the
string into an iridescent
trampoline. Inside they
spin tales in time and
place and the widow
connects the threads.

The trapped fly is
consumed. The rain
erases the tapestry.
The stories end.
We all disappear
into the silent whole,
shaped like a web
woven by a trans-
parent weaver.

Monumental

In Richmond I saw the Triangle of
Reconciliation, a monument to
the slaves who were captured, bought
and sold in the triangle from England
to Africa to Virginia. That profit
was seed for commerce in the
colony.

Two embrace in a symmetrical
stone statue. Trader, master,
slave reconciled. Somehow
I saw how that story is played
out in me. A slave to the
master of perfection, the triangle
of ego, shadow and self need
to integrate in a smooth
symmetrical embrace.

"There were unspeakable
horrors in the middle passage,"
read the commentary on
the plaque. To reconcile,
one must face the inner
enemy and love the horrible and
beautiful truth of being human.

The triangle reminded me
of this and helps heal.

I struggle to be free
like a child bouncing

on a bed. To be unfettered
like a hummingbird
flown free to taste
the nectar of the gods
in a honey suckle vine.
In Richmond, I tasted this
richness.

Paradox

"If it's not paradoxical, it is not true."
—Shunryu Suzuki

"A paradox is the truth standing on its head in order
to be seen."
—G. K. Chesterton

The ego is an either/or organ.
Its job is to differentiate. Paradox
dictates an either and-or
world. Black/white, true/false,
right/wrong, good/bad is the ego
split.

How difficult, that two things
can be true at once. How
expansive to live with non-
dual mind. Yin and Yang each
opposite copies the other within.
Truth is, tension, conflict, friction

between held opposites creates
heat for evolution and transformation.
Not everything that feels bad is bad.
Not everything that feels good is good.
Is that a good or bad thing?

Yes.

Inspiration

After a long, late walk,
my sons meet me on the
screened porch of the cottage.
We saunter down the lawn

with long necks and des-
cend the dock ladder into
the chilly lake. With
water chest deep we three

talk of music, sports,
and spirituality, not as
if there is any difference
among the topics—for

it's all spiritual: exercise,
beer, water, conversation.
And the implicit love...
made explicit, while

swans, geese, ducks, and
gulls swim and fly
stirring the air and water
the inspiration of the
mindful moment.

Second Nature

So what is the first
nature. Is it mother?
And the second? "It
is second nature to me
now, like breathing out and
breathing in." So crooned
the crooner... .

Breath is natural. Until
it is interrupted, so too
heartbeat. Shall we make
a covenant to never assume
that what is natural is
to be taken for granted? Can
we make that second nature?

Being Human

There are four cornerstones of the
human being. Humans are
bio/psycho/social/spiritual
beings.

If you want to touch
all four simultaneously, take a
hike in the woods with a
friend.

Bowl of Cherries

The cherry tomatoes in the
ceramic bowel glazed blue
sat on the butcher block
in the center of the kitchen.

It looked a bit like
a large pomegranate
cut in two. Red circular
seeds in the fruit womb.

Too much could be made
of the birth, resurrection
symbol. I was thinking
more about the red

ovals and the uneven
shape of the glazed container.
I thought too, that those
colors aroused my sensorium.

Oxford Boathouses

Stacked in wooden rows, the boats
seemed sadly separated from their oars.
Dry, sleek, still not complete
until their arms are locked into
their stable hulls

The Isis from London's Thames,
a narrow emerald ribbon, turns
just below the blue footbridge
and becomes one again at the Cherwell,
just a mile from the folly.

Some night soon when the
time has come the oarsman will
insert his wooden wand and row
away in the graceful rhythm
of the dark, smooth scull.

Light Lines
(For Jack Meanwell)

I watched Jack Meanwell paint
on a rainy day. Colors were his
gift. The rocks at Stoney Point
were the color of fruit. Apricots,
peaches, and plums were tossed
atop the sand. Behind the bridge
a splash of red: Was the sun setting
or rising? The horizon, a gray
glaze, salmon clouds ragged
behind leaning pines. He smelled
sweet and oily: paint and pipe
smoke.

We stood like man-dolls
with our heads bobbing from
side to side searching for what
was unseen.

His open hand held an invisible
brush as he spoke about the work.
The movements were masterful
and yet innocent like a child,
conducting an absent orchestra.
Talk filled time, but only the painting
spoke. Like some ancient alchemist

seeking some sublime spirit
from matter he mixed color
with more commitment than
conversation.

74

The day never ended, like the piece of work, it was simply abandoned, and left everything implied.

Self Analysis

Living in the rent house,
not knowing we were poor,
Dad traveled; he was a
territory man. He leased
what were known as "service
stations." Mother suffered.
In those days in small-
town Oklahoma they didn't
diagnose or treat depression.

The last of seven children, she
was separated from her mom.
Her dad was a clergyman, who
died when she was three. Idealized.
Dad gone, at five, I was her surrogate.
Only brother withdrew. No TV.
radio off, nighttime. I put
my head in her lap. She
stroked my hair, "I hope
when you grow up you'll
help people with their sad-
ness."

I am a priest. I am a psycho-
analyst. Jung says, "The
greatest burden of the child
is the unlived life of the parent."
Of course, it is more complicated
than that. No thing is one thing.
For every effect there are many
causes. Sometimes God calls
through our neurosis.

Dexterity

At an Inner Journey retreat
check-in, my colleague, Marv,
reflected on aging. "You know
those plastic bags you get at
grocery stores, to put your vegetables
in? The other day I was at the
store and couldn't separate the
opening of the bag."

Dexterity means physical
and mental agility. Derived
from the Latin, "dexeritas:"
it means "skillful." When
Marv told his story he put
his finger together miming
an invisible bag and rubbed
his finger tips as if attempting
to separate the sides of the sack.

Marv is a skillful, agile
storyteller, that is not
lost in age, only richer.

Zen Master

I had a dialogue with
a Buddhist monk last
eve. Paradox of Love, the
subject, but we were
the two subjects. There
was a mysterious energy
between us that permeated
the hall. The words fit
the mystical music:
compassion, detachment,
eros, philia, agape,
mindfulness, path,
practice, shadow, mind.

I ended by saying, "I
wish we had a word
for the love of a priest
for a monk." He re-
mained silent with an
inscrutable smile.

Sense

The day was stained gray.
Winter had barely begun
to bare the branches. Time
had changed, and so too,
the light. It was dark when
he left my office. His
depression had robbed
him of animation. Just
when he emerged from our
trellised walk, he felt the
late fall breeze cold upon
his cheek. All in a moment,
he knew he would be better.
All in a moment, he knew.

Middle School

Roxanne had a red stain
on her white pants when
in middle school. The boys
put red Jello in her chair.

The smear was a scarlet
letter of shame and humiliation.
Middle school. The boys bully and
tease because they know no other

way to connect. Girls are all
dressed up with no place to
go. Not an easy time. A good
adolescence is hard to find.

Maybe it is so difficult as
to not get stuck there. Some
never get out.

Newtonian Spirituality

For Charles T. Newton, Jr.

I imagine you there. You
are seated on your farm house porch in
Winedale, your favorite place on earth.
If love can make a sacred space,
this was your sanctuary.

I see smoke swirl about
your head like a spirit
that is holy. You came late
to your spirituality, but just
in time... just in the fullness

of time. Yours was not a senti-
mental or unctuous piety,
but the kind that saw, "heaven
in a wildflower." You found your
heart's eye, that helped you see the

extraordinary in the ordinary,
the miraculous in the mundane,
the sacred camouflaged in the
profane. You loved this world
and all it's wild life. You found your

place on the good green earth.
You loved your family, as you presided
from that porch. You cherished your
garden where the plants in
their honeyed heaviness held

God's wild grandeur. The
full bodied trees, comfortable
in their lot, were like you, deep
rooted in Lone Star soil.
I see you seated in your

chair smoking a fine cigar
cherishing your humble life
no longer in a hurry, going
no where, content to find
meaning in what you have.

Your life was finally in
focus to picture this. Your
life abundantly full, and
now complete - no brief,
no opinion, no final argument.

Just this: you peacefully
seated on your porch. Your
face has that tight-lipped
grin, beneath your burnt orange
cap, your eyes are now clear

and they see clearly that life
was worth it all. The suffering
built soul, the love
healed the pain and
new life will conquer

death. I see you seated
now on your farm house
porch. And then I don't.

I see your empty chair
there in your porch sanctuary

and you have stood straight,
shoulders back, head high, and
crossed into the other realm leaving
us to remember you with
undying respect...

For you died well,
you died very, very well.

Clementine

My great-grandfather was
one of three sons. My
grandfather was one of
two sons. My father
was one of three sons.
I am one of two sons.
I have two sons. Each
of them has a son.

Then,
Along came Clementine.
The feminine principle
personified. Curly long
hair. Will wear only
dresses. Flirts. Dances
to the Fresh Beat Band.

How refreshing, how
completing, how re-
newing. How mysterious.

Between the Lines

Some claim to be
able to read between
the lines. What could
that possibly mean?

Are they smarter, more
intuitive? By what
right do they have to
assume that they could

read another's mind
and not trust enough
to take him at his
word. Grandiose,

inflated. How dare
they read between
the lines. They probably
think I am insecure,

"reading between the lines."

Blue Hue

Two roses in a cut
glass vase, a perfect
scene for a few poetic
lines. Problem is the

color of the one is
between red and
orange. How tempting
to create a word

color: "rorange."
The problem is the
other rose is a
combine of white

and green. "Grite,"
doesn't work as well.
Rorange and grite roses,
long stemmed and

leaning against a
crystal vase. Problem
is the vase has a blue
hue. You take it from here.

Mirror

When Finn was three,
his dad delivered him
for a weekend stay. "Dad,
when Finn says he wants
to play 'car car,' he doesn't
want to push matchboxes
on the floor. He likes to
sit in a real car and
pretend he is driving.
Don't leave him alone."

I opened the garage door
to deposit the garbage. My
grandson saw my auto. "Play
car car!" I yielded to
his directions as he patted
the passenger side. He
stood behind the wheel,
reached forward, turned
on an invisible key. He
then flipped down the
visor, opened the
mirror, and with a
fluttering of tiny hands,
he fluffed both sides
of his hair. Then
pretended to put the car
in gear and back away.

Mighty Quinn

When Dylan wrote "Mighty
Quinn," I never thought
he would be my grandson.
James Quinton was born

bold. He walked early and
often. When he enters
a room, he leans into
the space with a body language:

"Here I am, get over it." He
greets me with a run across
the room and a head-butt.
Curious, climbing, and always

carrying an instrument for
hammering. Shoe, cardboard
rolls from paper towels, broom,
bat, whatever he can find to

hammer. At a year and
a half, he has a presence of
power. A blond and azure-
eyed boy of joy and laughter.

"Come all without. Come all within.
You'll not see nothing like the mighty Quinn."

        Amen

I'm Thinking

Baxter's eyes are cornflowers,
his hair honey. His mom
told him, "no more popsicles."
He found his grandmother

in the cottage kitchen. "I'm
thinking I want something
cold on a stick... ."

Another time, having been
told, "No more chocolate
chip cookies," he found his
father on the screened porch.
"I'm thinking I want some-

thing flat with chips on it."
Bax is three; I'm thinking
we have a creative mind:
thrilling and terrifying.

Daughter of God

Looking down, I placed the
white wafer in the pink palm
of a little girl. Pink and
white, sacramental flesh.

The sacrament was not in
the host alone, nor in the
hand held up. The sacrament
was in the integration of the two.

White circle in a pink palm.
Combined colors of the human
and divine integrated in
a simple Sunday scene,

never before, never again.
All in a moment, "infinity
in the palm of [her] hand."

Synchronicity

On a plane to officiate
at Bill Alley's funeral,
I read a poem by Raymond
Carver called "Hummingbird."

His wife Deborah loved the
poem and its sentiment.
After the reception following
the funeral, my wife and
I sat on our cottage's screened
porch, with a relaxing drink.

Three times a hummingbird
appeared suspended six feet
in front of us. Each time
it disappeared it returned,
hung before us with fluttering
wings. Finally, I said, "We

see you Bill." The tiny
one took wing. Mircea
Eliade says, "The animals
are the messengers between
the realms."

Synchronicity II

After Deborah Alley
heard the hummingbird
story, she took the name
"Waylala." It means humming-
bird in Cherokee. She
was mystical and ran a
fairy school for children.

After a decade of dancing
with cancer, she finally
let go. As with her husband,
Bill, I officiated at her
burial. At the homily,
I read the poem and told
the story of the humming-
bird and how she got her name.

After the funeral, her niece
ran to me: "A hummingbird
is trapped in our house."
Hummingbirds are messengers—
spirit symbols.

Note to Noted

When a young priest, I
wrote a note to noted
author/theologian, Frederick
Beuchner. I asked forgiveness
for all the plagiarizing I
had done of his good work
and thanked him for this
profound influence on my
theological world view.

By return mail on lined
paper from a legal pad he wrote:
"I was sitting by the sea, wondering
if the world wanted another word
from me, and your letter came."

Fall

I love the light this time
of year, how it bends and
seems more golden. Things
seem a bit slower. It is
fall. Interesting title for a
season. I suppose it de-
rives from what happens
to the leaves. There is no sound
that inspires me any more
than the crisp crack from
stomping through piles
of leaves. They were once
green, then golden, now
brown and fallen. May
be we name this season
after that other garden
and Fall.

Extraordinary in the Ordinary

One can sit for a cycle of
seasons and see the whole of
human nature in nature.
In the spring, watch a tree.
The knuckled bud on the branch
becomes a bloom and then a
blossom.

"April is the cruelest month."
All sorts of bulbs are dying
to be born, struggling to
crack the earth's crust. And
in due time, they all fall
down. So with us, "All
flesh is grass."
I choose to bloom where I
am planted if even for
a season.

There Aren't Many Adults

The young curate came to the
old rector as he lay
dying. "You have been
a parish priest for fifty
years. What do I need
to know from you?"

The old man said, "Things
are never as good as you
think they are going to
be, nor as bad. Not every-
thing that feels bad is bad,
not everything that feels good is.
And, there aren't many adults."

What is an adult?," said the
Curate. The wise old man opined,
"One who can control impulse and
delay gratification. One who knows
he can't have it all, and that there
ain't no magic other. He knows
that the secret to life is that there
is no secret and gives himself to
something greater than himself."

"Oh," said the purer priest and
paused, then he said it again, "Oh!"

Falling Star

The night Stuart Hellmann
died his son stepped out-
side. Glancing upward he
saw a shooting star flash
across the sky.

Stuart was a mentor
for me. Sounds like
meteor doesn't it?   That
night it was a falling star.

Amusing

Calliope was the muse of
epic poetry. Euterpe the muse
of lyric. Thalia comedy and
pastoral poetry. Erato, love poetry
and Polyhymnia, sacred poetry

Inspire means to have the
spirit enter one's soul.
So muse and inspiration have
a common task, to awaken
the creator in every creature.

My experience is that they
exist in a mysterious auton-
omy. When beckoned they
flee. When least expected
they descend or ascend as the

case may be. Updike says:
"In writing, necessity is a
virtue." So why wait to be
inspired by your muse? Sometimes
starting without them makes them
want to join in.

Our Promise

Someday the day will not end
and never die again.

It will be alive and full
for the first time and now just begun.

All that was, will now be
born delivered from the womb of time.

All matter will change to love.

And what for no reason was
will be, for some reason, evermore.

Bugged

In the mystery of calling,
who knows why I so love
words. The first time I heard
the word *archipelago* I
had to know what it meant.

Entomology is the study of
bugs. Etymology is for
those bugged by words. Word
sounds, sibilance is a hissing
sound. Onomatopoeia is
a word imitating a sound.

Hissing is onomatopoeia. First
time I heard that word, I had
to know what it meant.

Peaceable Kingdom

Hanging in the hallway of my
grade school was a print. Young
child, with an arm around the
mane of a lion and at his feet
were animals. A lamb and wolf;
a leopard and calf.

A 19th century Quaker, Edward
Hicks painted "Peacable Kingdom."
Isaiah: "The wolf shall dwell
with the lamb, and the leopard
with the kid and the calf and
lion... and the little child
shall lead."

Under that print, I saw my
friend Mary hobble the hall
with polio. Dio Daily split
his lip and bled a pool
below the scene. In the second
grade they told Michael Dougherty
that his mother had died.

A child and a lion, embracing
the wild and savage animal
we call life.

Light and Shadow

I wish you could see the light
and shadow on my office wall. There is
a wagon wheel rolling by a
tree. The shadow of leaves move
slowly from side to side behind
the dark spokes. The wall is cream,
the light pulls out the yellow in
the pigment and the color is enhanced.
One section looks like a grapevine
swaying on a dark wire. Even
in the time to write this poem,
the wagon wheel is gone, replaced
by a crocheted doile, like my
grandmother had on her table,
no, now it is the lace she
wore on the front of her dress.

Marc Chagall

My son and I meditated
before Chagall's "Windows
in Zurich." Picasso said
"Chagall must have an
angel in his head."

Floating angels, green
fiddlers, smiling pigs
were the creative genius's
media for mystery. The
artist's world view was

summed in his own
words: "In our life
there is a single color
on an artist's palette,
which provides the meaning

of life and art. It is the
color of love." Love
makes pigs smile.

He Was Killed on the Way to a Stop Smoking Class

It is said, "There ain't no
justice." Jesus taught, "The
rain falls on the just and
unjust."

A friend says, "I'm glad
life is not fair, or I'd
be dead." "I don't deserve
this! " I pray I never get what
I deserve.

Oklahoma Son

Granddad's Stetson halo rests
uncomfortably on devilish eyebrows,
a captured contradiction by Mother's
four photographs of her golden boy in
the Oklahoma sun.

Overalls pinstriped bare arms holding
temporary tattoos caught in an instant
for Mother's four photographs of her
golden boy in the Oklahoma sun.

Summer instant recorded for wet eyes
reflecting the passing age of a boy
child by Mother's four photographs
of her golden boy in the Oklahoma sun.

Country singer sings phrases and stages,
sounding natural frames for Mother's
four photographs of her golden boy in the
Oklahoma sun.

Loss of Innocence

Before ten I was given the mixed
blessing of a BB gun. The masculine
symbol was called "Daisy." Alone
with my androgynous instrument,

I looked for birds. In the top of a
small Chinese elm sat a smaller
brown sparrow. Like a lunar
tide some unknown force emerged.

Pressing the cheap metal against
my check, I had a choice and
I had no choice, but to pull the
trigger, a puff, and the bird fell.

Rushing to the broken sidewalk
beneath the tree of life I
saw death in a small
sparrow no larger than my hand.

I left the Garden that day.

Empty Steps

Monday morning early, I left in the
dark to travel to be with my
mother who was lying in a
hospital bed. As I turned from

the interstate, the day was
breaking, and fog was still
in the shallow valleys on east
Texas' edge. Buffalo, a town

of 1,500, so says the sign.
I was welcomed by the Rotary
Club, Elk's Club, churches and
the Home of the 1979 Bi-District Champs.

Caution light slowed me in a
school zone. Sitting on the
school steps was a boy of seven or
eight. He had a burr haircut.

He wore a long-sleeved, flannel
shirt, new blue jeans rolled up.
On his left was a #8 brown
lunch sack, folded neatly at the top.

On his right was a brand new,
blue, canvas covered, cardboard
three-ring binder. His daddy
dropped him early on his way

to the oilfield. I know that
little boy. I visited my mother
as she lay dying. I left her
on Thursday evening. I drove

through Buffalo. The school
steps were empty. It was
dark. The little boy had
disappeared. The next day

I awoke at sunrise.
It was dawn and I
was home.

Bad Theology

The late Urban T. Holmes tells
a story of a woman upset
with the new liturgy who scurried
up to him after the service.

"If our Lord were around
today and heard all of this
new-fangled abomination
in our precious Prayer

Book, he would roll
over in his grave!"

What is Missing

I have long known that what
is missing is most important.
The white space between words
is necessary to read a line.

In music, the pause and
silence are as profound as
the music and the words.

So too, it is with nails,
clamps, staples, unseen and
holding things together.
In a stained glass

window, as important
as the colored glass is
the dull gray lead which
makes a pattern and

holds it all together.

Paradox

"If my devils are to leave me,
I am afraid my angels will take
flight as well." —Rilke

How hard to hold a non-
dual mind: Garbage is
fertilizer. Suzuki pens:
"If it is not paradoxical, it's
not true." It seems against
nature to hold a paradox.
The worst thing that ever happened
to me was the best thing
that ever happened to me.
In this world, there are
not either/or, but either
and or.

Memory and Imagination

Keats writes, "When I have fears
that I may cease to be, before
my pen has glean'd my
teeming brain."

I'm not sure I share Keats'
fear, but words do flow with
occasional eddies, and
blockages. But it is not about
the words; it is about trying
to bring the mystery present
with memory and imagination
the bookends of experience.

And words are the wings
that carry the image
home, like sound angels
that flutter.

The Colonel

My brother died today.
I am 5 and he 7.
I wanted his attention
so badly as to make
a fool of myself, and
he consistently pointed
that out to me. I was
5 before I knew gum

was sweet. He would
tell me he wanted to
soften it first. We played
football and basketball

together. He better in
one, and I the other. We
did not compete, but
had each other's backs.

I cried when he left to
become a military man.
He was born a colonel in
the Air Force. His

medal for valor in
Vietnam brought
respect and pride.

We were like the
English tradition.

One son to Her Majesty's
military and the other

her church. I am an
imagineer, he an
engineer. We never
quite understood one

another but who under-
stands love? Creative,
male model military,
vulnerable, quiet,

wounded. I knew he
knew how much I
needed his approval.
I have it, his way.

My only brother died
today and a part of
me died too. My brother
got well today and
a part of me did
too.

The Corner of My Eye

While lecturing in Louisville
one Sunday morn, the room
was full and full of energy
that filled me with creativity.

The audience was the other
side of my muse. Out of
the corner of my eye I saw
a woman standing at the door.

She wore a trench coat
pulled tight and dark glasses.
Immediately I was attracted
to her presence. Not wanting

to be distracted, I looked
away. She traversed the back
wall crossing once again
into my line of sight.

A giggle of joy erupted in
me with the graceful and
grateful realization that
that was no mere woman, that was my wife.